THE LIGHTER SIDE OF HORSE MANURE

poems by

Linda Drattell

Finishing Line Press
Georgetown, Kentucky

THE LIGHTER SIDE OF HORSE MANURE

Copyright © 2024 by Linda Drattell
ISBN 979-8-88838-760-3 First Edition
All rights reserved under International and Pan-American Copyright Conventions. No part of this book may be reproduced in any manner whatsoever without written permission from the publisher, except in the case of brief quotations embodied in critical articles and reviews.

ACKNOWLEDGMENTS

Wingless Dreamer *Vanish in Poetry* anthology: "The Vet Who is also the Dentist"
Las Positas College *Havik* anthology: "I Imagine Him Saying Thank You"
Wingless Dreamer *Ink the Universe* anthology: "The Sparrow and the Oak"
Wingless Dreamer *Unveil Your Memories* anthology: "Clover"
Wingless Dreamer *Crystalline Whispers* anthology: "Squirrel Amnesia"
Viewless Wings/2024 Dublin Poetry Walk: "Compliment"

Publisher: Leah Huete de Maines
Editor: Christen Kincaid
Cover Art: Shawn Drattell
Author Photo: Monique Rardin Richardson
Cover Design: Elizabeth Maines McCleavy

Order online: www.finishinglinepress.com
also available on amazon.com

Author inquiries and mail orders:
Finishing Line Press
PO Box 1626
Georgetown, Kentucky 40324
USA

Contents

The Barn Manager Hates My Horse 1
Photo 3
The Water Trough 4
Home 5
At the Farm, Far From the Barn 6
Hooves 7
The Vet Who is also the Dentist 8
I Imagine Him Saying Thank You 10
The Ride 11
Emergency Supplies 13
Shifted Stance 14
Love Does Have Boundaries 15
Loose Shoe 16
Compliment 17
Lunging Vegas in the Corral 18
Clover 19
Chromatic Coupling 21
Squirrel Amnesia 22
The Sparrow and the Oak 23
A Horse's Guide to Seasons of the Year 24
Flies 25
I Bring You Grain This Evening 26
Quietude 27
Farewell to an Old Horse 28
Flying 29
Photo 30
Bio 31

The Barn Manager Hates My Horse

If he's going to stay here
you'll need to keep his stall clean
I'm not doing it
He knocks his grain out of the bucket
Then come the flies
I can't stand the flies
And he smells
He stands at my water trough all day rinsing
his mouth in the water—it's disgusting
You cost me insurance money
the minute you set foot on my property
The monthly fee I charge you is nothing
compared to what it costs me
Even if you're buying your own grain
Even if you don't ride him
It's a losing proposition
I offered you a place to keep him because
I think you're a nice person
His arthritis is bad
Nothing good can come
from taking care of that old horse
I've so many good memories of him
He's going to have a hard time over the winter
See, he's losing so much weight
Yeah, sometimes I don't feel like feeding him
Sometimes I don't let him out
I have younger, gentle horses for you to ride
Fifty dollars an hour
You can lease one of my horses
Time for you to let him go
I can transport him for you
The vet's very good at what he does
He won't feel a thing
I'm not ready

Well, then, get a shovel, pitchfork, and a rake.
Use the blue broom
It washes easily
Get all the loose grain
I don't want the flies—
You really love him, don't you?
Yes, I do

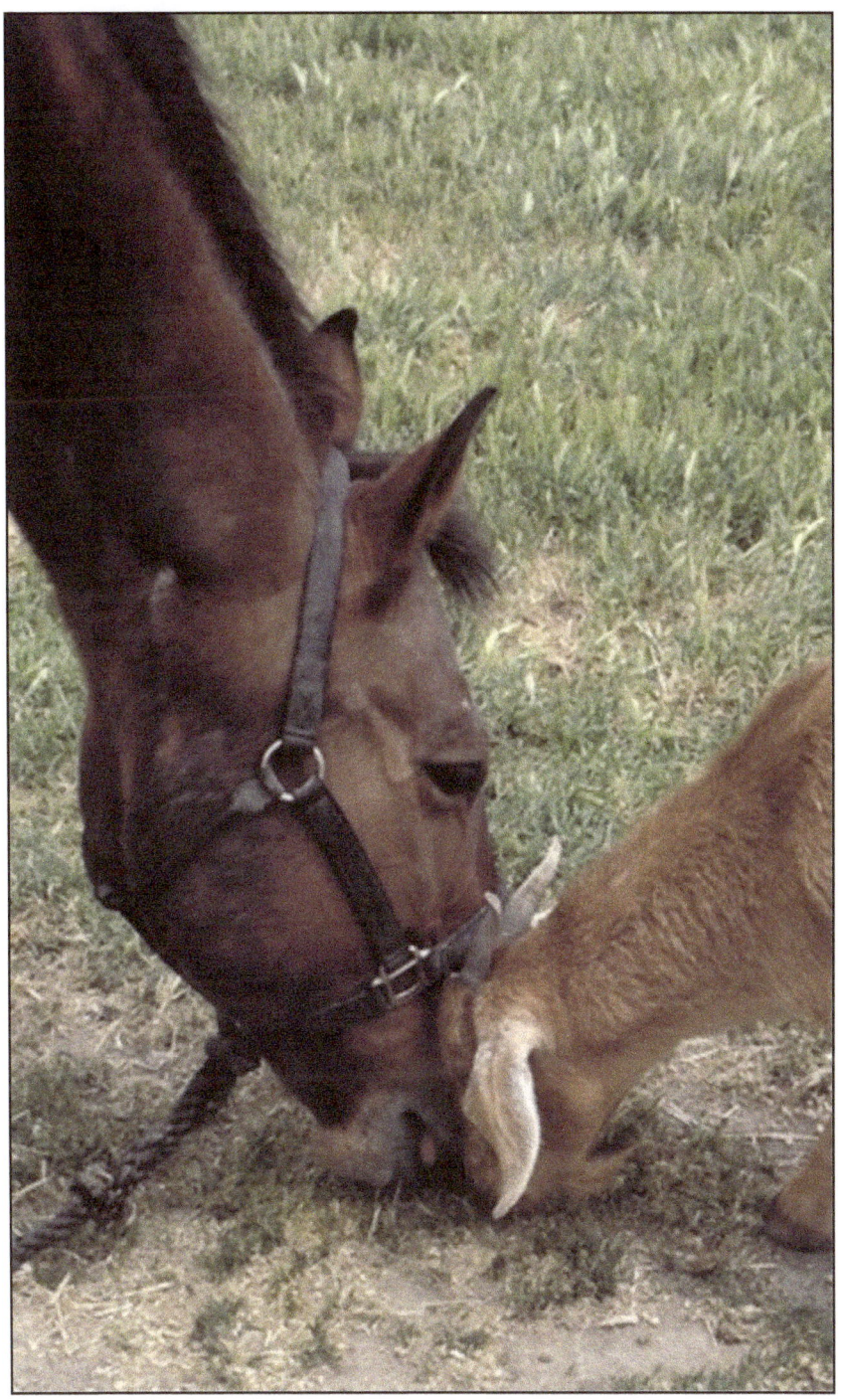

The Water Trough

Owner's late?
Stale hay you ate?
Caught your tail on the pasture gate?
Need a chance to commiserate?
Take it to the water trough.

Need to neigh?
Want to play?
Rather do nothing but laze all day?
Prefer pasture to stall, come what may?
Take it to the water trough.

Pass the time?
Escape the grime?
Your aches tell you you're past your prime?
Think doing nothing is not a crime?
Take it to the water trough.

We're all there—
Even the mare—
Whinnying our hearts out without a care—
But if you're sour don't you dare
Take it to the water trough.

Home

Home is pasture.
Wind caressing grasses
showcase vibrantly verdant hills.
Darting squirrels abounding.
Geese honking
mimic horses neighing.
Pigweed overrunning goldenrod.
Piled manure aging
near prepared compost.
Aging lone oak, steadfast.
Swallows swooping and
starlings murmuring beckon
clouds draped heavily.
Renovated barn is backdrop.
Trough full.
Peaceful ambience.
—Home—
Ambience peaceful.
Full trough.
Backdrop is barn renovated.
Heavily draped clouds
beckon murmuring starlings
and swooping swallows.
Steadfast oak lone, aging.
Compost prepared near
aging manure piled.
Goldenrod overrunning pigweed.
Neighing horses mimic
honking geese.
Abounding squirrels darting.
Hills verdant vibrantly showcase
grasses caressing wind.
Pasture is home.

At the Farm, Far from the Barn

The manure pile
If stood awhile
Becomes a nourishing food.
But used too ripe
Can kill in one swipe
One's garden and one's mood.

Hooves

Confined in his stall he waits with penned hooves,
The farrier's late to fix and mend hooves.

He hates being hemmed in, prefers to romp,
To stomp with his field mates, prance and wend hooves.

He craves the freedom to gambol and play,
To run with the herd, together blend hooves.

The farrier files and snips his hoof walls,
Applies her deft skills to trim and tend hooves.

After Fay's treated his feet he's released,
Freed, my horse runs, once again, to rend hooves.

The Vet Who Is Also the Dentist

Hmm,
Not my stall
Nicer wood
No kick marks like in mine
Shavings are clean
As if no one stays long enough to leave their calling cards
There's water
No hay
Ah, a vet visit
To what do we owe the pleasure?
Pat on my neck
Yeah, yeah, hello to you too
Now I'm in cross-ties
Why'd she do that
I'm not difficult
She says it won't hurt
Feel the prick of a needle
Ooooooooooooooh
Where was I
Hmmmmmmmmmm
So drowsy
What was in that needle
I'd love to lie down
She's asking my owner for help
Keeping me from hanging my head too low
But I can't help it
Go with the flowwwwwwww

The vet is putting a contraption around my mouth
Hey, get out of there
Cold metal against my tongue
Soapy taste
What the heck…
Gggrlrgggrrrrllllaaaaaahhhhhh
Not the teeth not the teeth not the teeth
I have very little left
What did I hear?
No more hay?
Forget the grass?
Like hell I will
Oh, I can have more sweet grain
Lots and lots and lots of grain
Well okay
I can live with that
Finally done
Wasn't too bad

I Imagine Him Saying Thank You

My horse gave me a funny look today
As if he felt he just had to say,
"Again, you carry my manure away
Such doggedness and care you display

And I want to ask you—Who gives a shit?

You watch me eat, measure my weight
Act enthralled to see that I ate
You ask, Enough? when I stare at the gate
Is this a natural human trait

Really, I ask you—who gives a shit?

We've one shot at life yet you share yours with mine
carrying buckets and shovels seems fine
I don't really care how you spend your time
But yes, without you, my health would decline.

So, thank you—now get on with your shit."

The Ride

There were ten of us who hit the trail,
Two leaders, then eight more
We traveled light
The strong and the frail
And AJ cried, "Nevermore, nevermore!"
And AJ cried, "Nevermore!"

We laughed and laughed and thought we were sane
Galloped, wishing to soar
AJ gripped mane
And as sunlight waned
Plaintively cried, "Nevermore, nevermore!"
And AJ cried, "Nevermore!"

Nine in saddles and AJ bareback
Four hours, then three more
As evening neared
We pulled on our tack
While AJ cried, "Nevermore, nevermore!"
And AJ cried, "Nevermore!"

Searching for home, we tried every trail
AJ complained, "I'm sore!"
We shook our heads,
As we chased our tails,
And AJ cried, "Nevermore, nevermore!"
And AJ cried, "Nevermore!"

Our leaders opined, "Loosen your reins!"
"Yes!" we cried to the fore.
"Let the steeds roam
They'll lead, no restraints!"
And AJ cried, "Nevermore, nevermore!"
And AJ cried, "Nevermore!"

Thanks to horse sense and brilliant advice,
We reached, oh, the barn door!
By our wise choice
Or throw of the dice.
And AJ cried, "Nevermore, nevermore!"
Dismounting, cried, "Nevermore!"

Emergency Supplies

It's been a long trail ride.
Five of us emerge from dense forest
and arrive at a delectable meadow.
The thick stretch of treetops yields
to a blue canvas where white wisps
of no consequence scatter about,
unobserved by our horses
whose laser focus is on the tender shoots
sprouting from the soil.

"I've become like my horse," I say,
"I see grass and I drool."
"I've a thing for clover," Mary says.
"Yes, clover," another says,
smacks her lips.

"Alrighty, out of curiosity," Mary asks,
what's everyone got in their saddlebags?"
"Hoof pick."
"Hoof pick."
"Hoof pick."
"Hoof pick."
"Lipstick…what?"
"Nuthin'," says Mary.

Shifted Stance

As arthritis kicks in and his hind legs stiffen,
my horse's affable attitude stiffens as well.

Vegas has developed an acerbic old man's crankiness,
a shrill whinny, a sharp refusal to follow simple requests.

On the other hand, imagine my surprise as I watch him
lift his right hind leg, turn his head gracefully, arch

a limber neck, extend his muzzle close to his hock
and inspect it—a show of flexibility I was never able

to get him to execute on command. He then lifts his left hind leg—
arches his neck again exquisitely to inspect that hock as well.

And to think I offered handfuls of carrots all these years
for an unenthusiastic half turn of the head.

Love Does Have Boundaries

My horse has lost his allure.
He's rolled in cow manure.
It's all over his mane,
which is twisted again,
his version of haute couture.

I stay away from his front
which, sadly, is gross, to be blunt.
He nuzzles my face;
I cry, *Personal space!*
He then passes gas with a grunt.

Loose Shoe

Jonathan, Harrington, Winifred too,
went for a ride till a horse threw a shoe.
"Oh no!" "Tough luck!"
"What can we do?"
cried Jonathan, Harrington, Winifred too.

One rode slowly, one followed in queue.
The third walked briskly, holding the shoe.
Back home to the barn
went the riders so blue,
their horses delighted—nothing to do!

Leaving their horses, the riders withdrew
To find another fine sport to pursue
The horses whinnied
triumphantly, "Whoo!"
as they munched on hay and made use of the loo.

Compliment

A woman was told,
"May I be so bold,
From the rear you resemble a horse."
"I am offended!"
"No offense intended,
I refer to your rich mane, of course!

Observed from behind
Equine tail comes to mind.
In awe, I'm inclined to compare.
A trait I do laud
Indeed I applaud
You would make a most beautiful mare!"

"Well, I do declare!"
"I refer to your hair!
No insult intended, my queen."
"You think I'm comely."
"No, you're quite lovely."
"Then, dammit, just say what you mean."

Lunging Vegas in the Corral
(feel free to sing along)

I've got the lunge line in my hand
I've got the lunge line in my hand
I've got the lunge line in my hand
The lunge line in my hand

It's you and me, Vegas, in this can
It's you and me, Vegas, in this can
It's you and me, Vegas, in this can
I've got the lunge line in my hand

To the left
To the left!
Dammit, I said, to the left!

I've got a lunge whip in my hand
I've got a lunge whip in my hand
I've got a lunge whip in my hand
A lunge whip in my hand

Good boy. Here's a carrot.

Clover

Darting ball of mocha fur,
speckled Nubian ears,
inquisitive face,
horns barely buds,
she'd jump on my back,
straddle her mother,
flop onto my beach chair,
press her forehead
against the mesh seat
to see what was up
on the other side,
even then a feisty goat.

When her horns grew
to the length of my thumbs,
she retreated from the butts
of raucous bucks,
glanced at me glumly.
Stick up for yourself, I said.
The herd is a rough place.
Her youthful eyes locked with mine,
then she turned and fought back,
head-butted everything in sight,
newest bully of the field.

That one,
the farm manager said,
shaking his head.
I found another farm,
then another,
and another.
Finally, a friend
with her own herd
an hour away
agreed to take her in.

Two bone curves
now crowned her head,
fully formed,
formidable.
She tried again
to bully her way,
rammed her head
against a fencepost,
broke both horns,
lost her edge,
a full-grown nanny banished
to the lowest rung
of the ladder,
her rank below
even that of the newborn
whose own head
was just busting buds.

No choice but to accept her place
in this newest herd.
My beautiful doe,
my Clover.
But, really,
it's her own fault.

Or is it mine?
Mindful mother that I was,
demanding she
stick up for herself.

Chromatic Coupling

Wild grasses
give way to goldenrod,
bright yellow specks carpeting the hills.

An outcropping of pigweed grows nearby,
circular green fans raised proudly on thin stems,
round leaves held up toward the sun despite their weight.

Two geese,
white balls of feathers with long thin necks,
dart across the field.

Blue-black barn swallows
fly out from the shed,
parading pale underbellies.

A skunk has entered a humane trap
meant to capture ground squirrels,
not realizing it can get out just as it got in.

White running dollups, black flying spots,
yellow specks, green circles,
and the black and white skunk no one wants to go near.

An exhibition of Pointillism,
everything separate,
everything connected.

Squirrel Amnesia

Skinny squirrel leaves his hut
Gnawing feeling in his gut
Lost a nut
What a rut
He regrets
When he forgets
Scratches his breast
Looks back at the nest
Sits on haunches
Clasps front paws then—l a u n c h e s
Retracing each step
Feeling inept
Where did he bury it
Oh—the hell with it

Going to be a long winter …

The Sparrow and the Oak

Sparrow called to Oak in plea,
"Let's swap places, you and me.
Consider the opportunity,
With your strength and vitality
An eagle I would be,
And you, with my agility,
Could as the beautiful willow sway.
Let's change places for just one day!"

Replied Oak to Sparrow,
"I, catch the beauty of the willow?
You, the path of an eagle follow?
This far-fetched fancy rings too hollow.
Instead of glory we might wallow
In quirky traits we'll have to swallow.
What if, instead, my wide roots you earn
And I, your feathers receive in turn?"

"Please, let's try,"
Said Sparrow, "How I'd fly!
"It's natural to reach for the sky.
Come now, let's agree, you and I."
"Hmm," Oak answered, with a sigh,
"Neither you an eagle nor a willow I.
Though the willow's plumed joy I would love to taste,
Fanned branches beckoning lovers' embrace.

All right, fine Sparrow, let's try our chances."
They swapped places, exchanged furtive glances.
Oak's trunk shriveled, his leaves thinned and fine—
To his chagrin, he became a pine.
And Sparrow's feet, with similar luck,
Grew wide and webbed as those of a duck!

A Horse's Guide to Seasons of the Year

Fly season
Fire season
Mud season
Dust season
Hay season
Grass season
Rainy season
Windy season
Shedding season
Too hot to ride season
Too wet to ride season
Too cold to ride season
Too nice to ride season
Get the hell off my back season

Flies

The horizon, a pastel sketch
of dry, dusty hills
and parched sycamore trees,
is dimmed by the thick haze
of smoke from distant wildfires.
I can barely see the golf course
on the other side of a desiccated depression
that used to be a creek until the county
put up a dam to create an artificial lake.
I can also barely see the lake.

I plan to lunge my horse in the round turnout.
These days Vegas moves at a measured pace
given the stiffness of his joints.
I let him run if he wishes, but lately
he foregoes a faster gait.
The hot noontime sun burns my eyes and nostrils
as much as it burns the sand in the turnout.
Vegas blinks to keep his own eyes moist,
tiny windshield wipers.
I should have come earlier, or later.
One benefit, though, no flies this time of day.

Vegas kneels, then rolls
to scratch an annoying itch,
rubs his back in the sand.
He rises, his caramel summer coat blackened
by a cloak of winged insects
wakened from their afternoon slumber
beneath the scorching crust of sand.
And here I'd always wondered where
the damned flies go to escape the heat.

I Bring You Grain This Evening

As I usually do
The breeze is warmer today
The ground is soft from a recent rain
Streaks of orange and pink blaze across the sky
The effect of water crystals in the upper strata, they say
What a beautiful sunset, I say

Your ebony mane has hints of henna
Soft to the touch and untangled
I call it the Woolite Effect
There's a fragrance to it of sweet citrus
I slide my hand from ears to withers over the crest
Just take a look at that sunset, I say

Your face is gaunt, you flatten your ears
Squint one eye as if harboring a stye
Nip at your chest suggesting flies out of reach
Lean to one side
Raise a leg up toward your belly, hold it there
You won't look at the sunset

You arch your neck, glance back at your torso
Assuming I'll follow your gaze
I glance up at the sky, assuming you'll follow … my gaze
But you don't, you're pointing out what's important to … you
And I—all right, anything else?
Forget the sunset

Quietude

My horse converses with a sharp look,
a flare of the nostrils, a swish of the tail,
a scratch at the earth with his hoof.

Cataracts have not dulled his ability
to convey his point of view.
He shakes his head, fires up his mane

from his poll to his withers,
reminding me he still has an attitude.
And yet—his calm gaze, his soft muzzle

against my cheek, the slow exhale
when I scratch behind his ears—
all convey something else.

Farewell to an Old Horse

I gave your lead rope to the vet
the toughest thing I've had to do
It meant I may still be there yet
no longer, though, in care of you

You wouldn't eat the grain I brought
Hard thing it is to say goodbye
A door will shut, last battle fought
We glanced and caught each other's eye

You rubbed your head against me, love
then turned aside and walked away
Don't follow me, I'm going, love
Yes, even if you choose to stay

Farewell, my friend, the pain's too much.
I'll miss your cheek, your muzzle's touch.

Flying

Put your boots on
One by one,
We'll go flying
When you're done.

About the Author

Vegas was only five years old when he met Linda, and it was love at first sight for both. Known for biting and having an incorrigible attitude (Vegas, that is)—his previous owner was terrified of him, the vet hated him, other horse owners avoided him—he greeted Linda every time she arrived at the barn with a soft muzzle and satisfying pffbbbffbbffbbbbbb. They enjoyed rides together, suffered dressage lessons together, and went on competitive trail rides (they both forgot at times that these rides were competitive and simply enjoyed the view). Vegas was prone to grabbing corn stalks as they passed fields and chewing them slowly as if he were an old hand with a toothpick. After more than 29 years together, Linda bade farewell to Vegas when he passed on to greener pastures in 2022.

But on to the rider! **Linda Drattell** is an award-winning poet and writer whose poetry and short fiction have appeared in both online publications and anthologies. Her poetry collection, *Remember This Day* (Finishing Line Press), was awarded the 2024 Bronze Award from Reader Views. Her co-authored children's book, *Who Wants to be Friends With a Dragon?* (Dorrance Publishing Company), received a Distinguished Favorite Award from the 2024 Independent Press Awards. *The Lighter Side of Horse Manure* and Linda's background with horses were featured on the Horse Chats Podcast. An excerpt from her unpublished novel, *The Peccadilloes of Filamena Phipps*, was a finalist and published in *Embark Literary Review*.

Linda holds an MBA from the American University and serves on the boards of the California Communications Access Foundation and California Writers Club/Tri-Valley Writers Branch. She may be reached on X and LinkedIn through her handle @LindaDrattell. Please visit her Facebook page, AuthorLindaDrattell, her website, www.LindaDrattell.com, and her Youtube channel: https://www.youtube.com/@LindaDrattell.

Linda has not yet decided whether her riding days are over. She is still mulling it over.

www.ingramcontent.com/pod-product-compliance
Lightning Source LLC
Chambersburg PA
CBHW040308170426
43194CB00022B/2943